5.95

Death and Resurrection
in Guatemala

Death and Resurrection in Guatemala

Fernando Bermúdez

*Translated from the Spanish
by Robert R. Barr*

ORBIS BOOKS
Maryknoll, New York 10545

The Catholic Foreign Mission Society of America (Maryknoll) recruits and trains people for overseas missionary service. Through Orbis Books Maryknoll aims to foster the international dialogue that is essential to mission. The books published, however, reflect the opinions of their authors and are not meant to represent the official position of the society.

Originally published in 1985 as *Cristo muere y resucita en Guatemala,* Voces Cristianas Latinoamericanas, no. 2, copyright © by Casa Unida de Publicaciones, S.A. (CUPSA), Mexico City, and Tierra Nueva, Buenos Aires, Argentina

English translation © 1986 by Orbis Books, Maryknoll, NY 10545

Scriptural quotations are from the Jerusalem Bible.

Manuscript editor: Mary Heffron

Library of Congress Cataloging in Publication Data

Bermúdez, Fernando.
    Death and resurrection in Guatemala.

    Translation of: Cristo muere y resucita en Guatemala.
    1. Persecution—Guatemala—History—20th century.
2. Guatemala—Church history.   3. Guatemala—
Politics and government—1945-   4. Bermúdez,
Fernando.   I. Title.
BR625.G9B46813   1986   209'.7281   85-48305
ISBN 0-88344-268-X (pbk.)

To the memory of my unforgettable friend,
Rubén Torres—"Bayron,"
a young Guatemalan Christian
murdered October 14, 1982,
and to that of the numberless martyrs of Guatemala
and all Central America
who have poured out their blood
for the building of a new society

I beg everyone to learn the truth and tell it to others. We must break the blockade of silence and lies. Let denunciation and proclamation take wings; let the bad news of death and the good news of resurrection in the lives of our Central American brothers and sisters be blazoned forth. May their blood—their poor, magnanimous blood—fall on our hearts and become Eucharist.

MONSIGNOR PEDRO CASALDÁLIGA
BISHOP OF SÃO FÉLIX, BRAZIL

CONTENTS

PREFACE

Central America today is a church of martyrs. Thousands of Christians in recent years have passed the supreme test of love, from Archbishop Oscar Arnulfo Romero, to the dozens of priests and ministers who have given their lives for their faith, to the countless catechists and members of the base communities who have done the same.

In this little book, I shall concentrate exclusively on a forgotten country of Central America—Guatemala. I shall attempt to present the witness of faith, hope, and love of Guatemala's heroic people in such a way as to offer a memorial to their martyrs, and to let my readers know the whys and wherefores of the situation of death in which they lived and died.

I should also like these pages to be a celebration—a celebration of the cause for which so many Guatemalan men and women have shed their blood, a celebration of the love that gives meaning to their death.

The memory of the martyrs is a call to solidarity with a struggle for life being waged by a whole people. We Christians see in this struggle the drama of Christ on the cross, the challenge to death that Christ hurls from a cross of injustice, poverty, oppression, and genocide. But we also see, in this same struggle, the clear sign of a resurrection.

It has been my happy lot to share the gift of faith over a

number of years with the *campesinos* in northern Guatemala. I came to them with the intention of evangelizing them, but they evangelized me.

I bless you, Father, Lord of heaven and of earth, for hiding these things from the learned and the clever and revealing them to mere children. Yes, Father, for that is what it pleased you to do [Lk 10:21].

The indigenous communities of Guatemala are teaching us what we cannot learn in books or in the halls of theological scholarship. They are teaching us what it means to share, what it means to trust in God, what it means to live as a Christian and be a Christian, what it means to give our lives for our sister and brother.

How many Catholic priests and Protestant ministers have paid the price of martyrdom in Central America for their determined commitment to walk with the people in their aspirations for a more just and humane society!

The reason the people of Central America struggle—as in Guatemala, where the vast majority are Amerindian Christians—is not communism, but the injustice of economic, social, and political inequality, the injustice of a situation of oppression and repression. Innumerable socioeconomic studies from various sources attest to this fact, as do certain groups of Protestants and Catholics. The bishops of Guatemala, for example, declared: "The violence in Guatemala is the fruit of an unjust social and economic system" (*Excélsior*, Mexico City, September 5, 1984).

Clearly, the native population has fallen into the hands of the mighty and the powerful, who have harassed, despoiled, outraged, tortured, and put them to death by the thousands. The cry of a people has come to the ears of the Lord. We Christians throughout the rest of the continent cannot simply pass them by, as did the religious individuals in the Parable of the Good Samaritan.

We discern a new spirituality arising out of this painful experience on the part of so many Christians—a new manner of following Jesus, of being his disciple, in a context of suffering. This new way of following the Lord Jesus flies in the face of the traditional manner in which so many, Catholics and Protestants alike, have sought to follow him. Beyond all doubt, our lives will be the richer for having studied at the feet of this suffering church, for having studied the experiences of its people in solidarity and shared commitment.

The purpose of the following testimonials—some of them documented by others, some the statements of persons with whom the author has spoken—is to alert the general public to the immense suffering of a people who hunger and thirst for justice and to enable them to share their mighty faith and hope. In spite of everything, this is a people of unshakable trust in the promises and the power of the Lord Jesus. As one of our brothers declared when he was on the point of death: "I'm going to die . . . but I know I'll rise again."

No, those who have the political, economic, and military power do not have the last word. The last word belongs to Jesus Christ, Lord of history, who is dying and rising at this very moment in the Guatemalan people.

SOME FACTS ABOUT GUATEMALA

Following are some official data regarding Guatemala:

Area: 42,042 sq. miles

Population (1985): 8.34 million, of whom more than 60% are indigenous Mayas

Rural population: 67%

Unemployment and underemployment: 45% of the work force

Illiteracy: 71% (in total population); 84% (among Amer-indians)

Infant mortality: 7.37%

Housing: Shortage of more than 900,000 units (1980). Of existing units, 57% are without drinking water, 72% without electricity, and 59% without sanitation.

The UN Commission on Food and Agriculture states that four out of every five peasant families in Guatemala live in destitution or near-destitution.

Government cuts in health and education budgets for 1984 were 20.8% and 15.5%, respectively. Military expenditure went up by 40%.

GUATEMALA

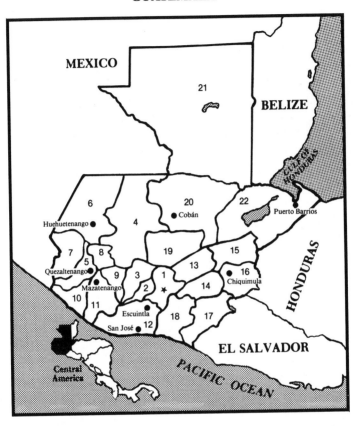

Central:
1. Guatemala
2. Sacatepéquez
West:
3. Chimaltenango
4. El Quiché
5. Quezaltenango
6. Huehuetenango
7. San Marcos
8. Totonicapán
9. Sololá

South:
10. Retalhuleu
11. Suchitepéquez
12. Escuintla
East:
13. El Progreso
14. Jalapa
15. Zacapa
16. Chiquimula
17. Jutiapa
18. Santa Rosa

North Central:
19. Baja Verapaz
20. Alta Verapaz
North:
21. El Petén
22. Izabal

★ Guatemala City

INTRODUCTION
by Phillip Berryman

This little book is a cry from the heart, an agonized cry in the name of the suffering people of Guatemala. Fernando Bermúdez, a priest who worked pastorally amid the violence in Guatemala until he had to flee to Mexico, is giving voice to the victims of that overwhelming violence. At the same time he is sharing with readers the faith and courage of the Guatemalan people and his conviction that ultimately they will not be vanquished.

Bermúdez points out that Guatemala is a "forgotten" country. In fact, the level of human suffering in Guatemala is as high as or higher than in El Salvador—recent data indicate that from 50,000 to 75,000 people have been killed since 1978—yet that suffering rarely reaches the U.S. media. There seem to be two main reasons: first, in the 1980s, there appears to be far less direct U.S. government involvement than in El Salvador and Nicaragua, and second, violence in Guatemala seems to be perennial and hence only the most bizarre cases are deemed newsworthy.

To appreciate the selective vision of the U.S. media, consider the killing of Father Jerzy Popieluszko in Poland, which became a daily media drama: his disappearance, the finding of his body, the trial of his murderers. Yet, with regard to Guatemala, the media have largely ignored the murder of about a dozen priests, several Protestant ministers, a Christian brother and a 50-year-old Guatemalan sister—without the slightest call to bring anyone to justice.

In his unpretentious little book, Bermúdez seeks to break through that indifference. He wants the world to know about the agony of the Guatemalan people. He is also convinced that their sufferings are the birth pangs of something very important for the life of the church.

Readers who go directly to the text will feel the impact of this account of brutality and courage. However, such readers might be left with a number of questions. Why does the Guatemalan army engage in atrocities: mass killings, bashing babies to death, gang-raping women in the presence of their families? How did church leaders among Guatemalan Indian peasants come to be perceived as such a threat?

In Mexico, where the original version of this book was published, the newspapers cover Guatemala and Central America much more extensively and with much more insight than do the U.S. media. Furthermore, many of the intended readers in Mexico have already met Guatemalan refugees and heard their stories. United States readers, however, who are much less familiar with the events mentioned here, may need some orientation. Hence, in what follows I will sketch some basic background elements of the Guatemalan situation.

Habitual stereotypes are one obstacle to understanding. For example, we may assume that the normal state of Guatemala's Indians is a kind of idyllic isolation until it is broken by the advent of tourism. We may view them as a people without history. Far from being historyless, however, the Indians of Guatemala have lived a history of oppression for over four centuries. Indeed their colorful clothes—admired by tourists today—were imposed on them by the conquerors in order to denote the wearers as being inhabitants of particular towns, towns the Spaniards themselves set up for the Indians. The patterns were taken from the Spanish courts. In other words, the picturesque Indian clothes were originally a means of social control.

Since the Spanish conquest the elites have monopolized the best lands for agroexport and have found ways of forcing the Indians to labor on their plantations. Indians were also forced to provide free labor for road-building and other government projects even after Independence (1821). When the Liberals took power in 1871, they immediately set out to cultivate coffee in order to supply the burgeoning demand in Europe, then in the midst of a major industrial expansion. They passed a law making it illegal to hold land communally, aiming at both the Indians and the Catholic religious orders. The law was justified on the grounds that both those "backward" groups stood in the way of "progress," namely coffee cultivation and export. Liberalism provided an ideological justification for a land grab. Not only were their lands taken away; the Indians were legally bound to work on the plantations a given number of days a year and to carry identification papers as proof that they had fulfilled their requirement.

Other handy stereotypes are those of the priest, the landholder, and the military officer, all part of the same oppressive system. Priests did tend to preach a static social order, wherein the poverty of some and the wealth of others reflected "God's will." However, this stereotype glosses over the fact that from the middle of the last century into this century, Liberal governments were at odds with the Catholic Church, passing laws to weaken it and taking away its property. Many of the clergy left the country and sometimes even bishops were expelled. The result was an institutional weakening of the church. Today approximately 80 percent of the priests in Guatemala are foreigners.

As a result of this institutional weakness, people living at the village level saw priests only rarely, on ritual occasions. Hence, a static and fatalistic religious worldview was transmitted through the culture itself: through parents and grandparents, legends and stories, prayers and proverbs.

Since Independence (1821), dictatorship has been the norm in Guatemala. Manuel Estrada Cabrera, who was in power from 1898 to 1920, and who was overthrown after being declared insane, served as the model for the book *El Señor Presidente* by the Nobel-prize-winning Guatemalan novelist, Miguel Angel Asturias. Then, in the 1930s and 1940s, when all Central American countries but Costa Rica were under dictatorships, came Jorge Ubico. Ubico was overthrown by a largely urban and middle-class revolt in 1944. From then until 1954 Guatemala enjoyed its only period of what might be called democratic rule.

The governments of Juan José Arévalo (1945–50) and Jacobo Arbenz (1950–54) were populist and explicitly sought to carry out a capitalist modernization in Guatemala. But Arbenz incurred the wrath of the Eisenhower administration because of his land reform program, which affected the United Fruit Company, the largest landholder in the country, and because he extended political freedom to the Communist Party.

The Arbenz reforms were largely carried out by the urban middle class, and Indians were generally not actively involved, with some notable exceptions. When Archbishop Rossell began to rally antigovernment sentiment in the name of anticommunism, he was able to appeal to the religious sentiments of the Indians.

Meanwhile, the CIA and the Eisenhower administration engaged in a multilevel destabilization effort, seeking to isolate Guatemala internationally and engaging in psychological warfare (e.g., flying over Indian towns and dropping copies of Archbishop Rossell's pastoral letter on communism). The CIA helped bring together a small group of what today would be called *contras*. When the invasion came, CIA-piloted planes bombed and strafed Guatemala City. Arbenz's officers, whose loyalty had been undermined by the United States, refused to support him, and he resigned. The new president, Carlos Castillo Armas, was flown to Guatemala on a U.S. embassy plane. Land reform was reversed, about two hundred "communists" were killed and hundreds more were arrested (the U. S. embassy supplied lists), labor unions were disbanded, and Guatemala entered its long night of violence.

During the Arbenz period the Catholic Church had begun a process of institutional rebuilding. This process was accelerated as relations with the Castillo Armas government warmed up. For example, several priests served in the National Assembly that wrote the country's new constitution. Soon, in response to the appeals of Pius XII and John XXIII, clergy and religious were arriving from Europe and North America. The Spanish Sacred Heart Fathers took charge of the Quiché area, which figures heavily in Bermúdez's narrative. The Maryknoll Fathers, who were increasing their presence in Latin America after being expelled from China, took responsibility for Huehuetenango.

Reflecting their pre-Vatican II mentality, this generation of missionaries came with a strong anticommunist thrust.

However, the Council and the growth of their own critical awareness of the conditions of the people led them to new forms of work such as the promotion of cooperatives and lay leadership training. Maryknoll pioneered in the formation of catechists, and the Sacred Heart priests developed Catholic Action, both forerunners of "basic Christian communities," with their lay leaders.

During the 1960s a guerrilla movement arose, concentrated largely in northeastern Guatemala, away from the Indian highlands. For a time this movement was apparently successful. Then, from 1966 to 1968, the Guatemalan army, under the command of Colonel Carlos Arana, unleashed a savage counterinsurgency campaign. Two aspects of this period are worth noting. First, the United States was intimately involved, funding and training the Guatemalan army, sending advisors, and by some accounts, even flying combat missions. Second, the president during this period, Julio César Méndez Montenegro (1966–70), was the only civilian head of state in over thirty years (1954–85), and as a condition for taking office, he had to guarantee the army a free hand in security matters. Under his nominal rule, 6,000 to 8,000 peasants were killed in order to stamp out a guerrilla movement that never numbered more than 300 combatants. This experience made Guatemalans skeptical about the significance of the election of a civilian president in 1985.

In 1967 Maryknoll priests Tom and Art Melville and Maryknoll Sister Marian Peter were beginning to collaborate with the guerrillas and planning to go to the mountains with them when they were discovered and denounced to Cardinal Casariego and the Guatemalan government and had to leave the country. The "Melville affair," like the death of Camilo Torres in combat in Colombia the previous year, dramatized a radicalization taking place in pastoral workers and alarmed the Guatemalan power structure. What Bermúdez describes in this book, however, reflects a much deeper grassroots process.

Colonel Arana became president in 1970. Although the guerrilla movements had been stopped, the pattern of killing continued with a wave of death-squad style repression in the cities. Since that time at least a thousand people a year have been routinely murdered for political reasons. The victims are primarily peasants, those who are considered to be leaders—including health promotors and catechists—and workers, especially those active in labor unions, as well as activist students and professional people.

After the earthquake of February 1976 a new cycle of grassroots organizing and pressure began, this time spearheaded by the labor movement. The Castillo Armas counterrevolution had reduced the organized portion of the work force from 10 percent to 2 percent, but now deteriorating living conditions and income, a result of the earthquake and the accompanying inflation, made people bolder in organizing to demand their rights. The labor movement became more militant and cohesive and new unions were formed.

During the previous decade church workers had been doing the kind of pastoral work endorsed by the Medellín Conference in what came to be called the "option for the poor," evangelization and *concientizacion* (consciousness-raising) in "base communities." This was by no means true everywhere, but notable were the diocese of Quiché, some parts of Huehuetenango, some parts of the agroexport area of the Pacific Coast, and numerous parishes in Alta Verapaz, Izabal, and the Petén, that is, areas to the east and north of the highlands. About half of the bishops were supportive of this kind of pastoral work in their dioceses, but Cardinal Casariego of Guatemala City managed to thwart the bishops' efforts to speak with a strong national voice. Consequently, in 1977, priests, sisters, and lay Catholics, along with a significant number of Protestants, formed the Committee for Justice and Peace. This organization functioned as a kind of network and rallying point for the defense of human rights. In 1978 Justice and Peace members were marching as a group in demonstrations. Hence, church people, catechists, priests and sisters, became targets for official violence.

Early in his account Bermúdez indicates that the core cause of the conflict in Guatemala is poverty generated and maintained by unjust structures. At this point we should consider this perception a bit more explicitly. The conventional view of Central America, such as that of the 1984 Kissinger Commission Report, tends to point to the country's 6 percent rate of growth during the 1960s and 1970s, though admitting that the wealth was shared unevenly. Those espousing this view see the crisis as originating in the economic recession of the later 1970s, which Marxists could exploit. They do not see that the very development model that brought "growth" also brought worsening conditions for many—if not most—people. As the coffee elites expanded into cotton, sugar, beef, and other products starting in the 1940s, they took land that could have been available to peasants. Hence, peasants had less land, and production of basic foods, such as beans and corn, declined on a per capita basis.

To illustrate with some figures of the 1970s: The official minimum wage for agricultural labor in Guatemala was slightly over a dollar a day. Yet prices were close to those in the United States: eggs, 80 cents a dozen; milk, 35 cents a quart; rice or beans, 25 cents or so a day per person. Subsistence peasants, of course, raised most of their own food, but for cash needs they had to migrate to the Pacific Coast to do seasonal labor. Expenses like prescription medicines could devastate a family's income.

Income in Guatemala is skewed: 2 percent of the population receives 25 percent of the national income: 50 percent receives only 10 to 15 percent. That top 2 percent has an average income *fifty times* that of the lower 50 percent, yet those who do the labor on the plantations that are the source of the wealth are precisely the impoverished lower 50 percent, primarily Indians. Life expectancy among Indians is 44 years—compared to 59.2 years for non-Indian Guatemalans and over 70 years for people in the United States. As Bermúdez rightly insists, the root cause of today's conflict in Guatemala is that poor people have stood up for their elemental right to live and have been met with violence. In desperation, some have turned to counterviolence.

In the early 1970s, small groups of survivors of the 1960s guerrilla movements quietly returned to Guatemala after devoting considerable time to analyzing what had gone wrong in the 1960s. In 1972 one such group entered El Ixcán, a remote northern lowlands area with no roads. These guerrillas would eventually call themselves the Guerrilla Army of the Poor (EGP), but at first they spent about three years simply learning how to live in the jungle and how to relate to the people settled there. Finally, as its first public action, the EGP "executed" a plantation owner notorious for his brutality toward his workers. In retaliation, the army rushed to the area and

rounded up thirty-seven local peasant cooperative leaders. Many of them were catechists, since a priest had
played a major role in starting the colonization project.
They were never seen again.

From that point on the army frequently kidnapped,
tortured, and "disappeared" Indian peasant leaders it sus-
pected of being "subversives." By the late 1970s dozens of
Indians in Quiché had been abducted and were never
heard from again.

The EGP carried out a number of symbolic actions.
Once in a cotton-growing area on the Pacific Coast they
burned over twenty crop-dusting planes to dramatize the
fact that overspraying and the growers' complete disre-
gard for safety regulations made thousands of workers
sick and caused perhaps hundreds of deaths a year. On
Sunday morning, January 20, 1979, the EGP moved into
an offensive phase, occupying the town of Nebaj for several hours. As they gave speeches explaining their position, the townspeople could see that most of the guerrillas
were Indians like themselves, speaking Ixil or Quiché.
Subsequently the EGP occupied dozens of towns and
villages in similar propaganda actions.

The most effective recruiting agent for the guerrilla
groups was the brutal Guatemalan army itself. At the
village level many people passed through various phases:
from consciousness-raising (often a result of pastoral
work), through projects, through a more militant organization, such as the Committee for Peasant Unity, to a
growing sympathy with the guerrilla movements, to col-
laboration (giving food or information on the army's
movements), and finally to active involvement as members. From the viewpoint of the people all this was experi-
enced as an act of collective self-defense. The traditional

communal way of thinking and acting of the Indians also meant that a process of this type and the decisions it entailed tended to be more collective than they might have been elsewhere. A whole village might go through such a process. No doubt the news of the successful overthrow of the Somoza dictatorship in 1979 and the growing opposition movement in El Salvador also gave the movement momentum.

For its part, the Guatemalan army increased its level of brutality step by step. In May 1978, for example, when a group of about a thousand peasants came to see the mayor of the town of Panzos to discuss a land dispute, troops and landowners opened fire and over a hundred peasants were killed (an event scarcely noted in the media, which in fact reported only the government's version). In late 1981 and especially in 1982, a full-fledged policy of mass killing developed. On the basis of its intelligence reports, the army determined which villages were organized or sympathetic to the guerrillas and pursued a deliberate policy of massacre. The army itself admits that 440 villages were destroyed. Approximately 50,000 Indians were relocated to "model villages," like the "strategic hamlets" of Vietnam, and up to one million (out of a total population of seven million) were displaced from their homes. One hundred thousand have fled to Mexico.

In the short run, the army's "counterinsurgency" was successful in the sense that the guerrilla organizations no longer pose a direct threat. Far from solving the underlying problems of the country, however, counterinsurgency aggravates them. The struggle is far from over.

The foregoing provides some information on developments leading up to the period covered in Bermúdez's narrative. We may now pass on to some observations on the account itself, which is organized not chronologically but by theme.

Assuming some familiarity with the situation on the part of the readers, the author in chapter one goes to the heart of the matter. He provides examples of the slaughter, in particular the massacre of about 350 people on July 17, 1982, in San Francisco Nentón, Huehuetenango. People are killed, says Bermúdez, because they defend their right to life.

Post-Vatican II Catholicism has seen a flowering of lay ministries in many places, stimulated in part by diminishing numbers of full-time priests. In Guatemala, however, as chapter two attests, because priests have been prevented from a normal ministry, a catacomb-kind of clandestine ministry has developed. In 1980, after two priests had been murdered, grenades had been thrown into a mission compound, and the bishop had narrowly escaped an ambush, the personnel of the diocese, of Quiché decided to close the diocese. Since then lay leaders have presided over worship services. Sometimes they journey to neighboring dioceses for clandestine meetings. Bermúdez relates that they sometimes carry the Eucharist back to their villages hidden among tortillas.

Since about 1981 some Guatemalan Indians have lived in *poblaciones en resistencia*, groups of people who refuse to come down to the army's "development poles" or "model villages"—a euphemism for a kind of concentration camp—and who are likewise unwilling to flee to refugee camps in Mexico. At one time there were as many as 40,000 Guatemalans living such a nomadic existence, on the move in sparsely populated areas. Today the number is probably less. Among these groups prayer and Bible reflection led by lay people continue to be important. Many feel that these groups, sharing privations, danger, and a fierce determination—"holding all things in common"—are the seed of a new church and even of a new society in Guatemala.

Chapter three is a martyrology: stories of a number of catechists who were murdered, followed by a series of priests and ministers. Note that Fernando Hoyos, who had spent many years as a Jesuit working with peasant groups, was killed as an EGP combatant. Does Bermúdez omit this fact purposely? My interpretation is that he sees all those who give their life for the people as martyrs, witnesses to faith and to life. That some do so as combatants does not eliminate the dimension of martyrdom.

Some Americans became aware of the slaughter in Guatemala after the March 1982 coup, which led to the presidency of General Efraín Ríos Montt, a born-again Christian. Chapter four presents accounts of some of the more gruesome killings that took place under his presidency. Chapter five, dealing with refugees, again gives accounts of the people's need for worship and prayer.

Bermúdez has already described unspeakable levels of cruelty. Yet in chapter six he goes even further, relating an occasion when the army forces members of a village to hack five young men to death or see the whole village slaughtered. The young men consent and even urge the others to comply so as to avoid a greater evil. This motivates the author to make a biblical reflection on the meaning of martyrdom.

What are we to make of Bermúdez's account? Some might dismiss it as propaganda, as an exaggerated and partisan document. Yet what Bermúdez relates is supported by the reports of human rights organizations such as Americas Watch, Amnesty International, and the UN

Human Rights Commission. We have here not a systematic overview but the witness of a pastor who has personally observed both the forces of death unleashed and the people's steady courage and determination.

In 1985 two anthropologists, Chris Krueger and Kjell Enge, did a survey of the results of several years of counterinsurgency in Guatemala. They concluded that the previous estimate that 20,000 to 50,000 people had been killed since 1978 was low; the true figure was 50,000 to 75,000. They arrived at these figures using the Guatemalan government's own survey of how many children had lost one or both parents. In other words, the level of human suffering in Guatemala is as high as or higher than that in El Salvador.

We noted above that one reason for the media's low level of interest in Guatemala is that U.S. involvement there is less than elsewhere in the region. In one sense that is true, but it is important to keep in mind that it was the U.S.-organized 1954 coup that installed the military/ oligarchical ruling group. The United States was heavily involved in equipping, training, and funding the Guatemalan army in the 1960s, and thus is largely responsible for the counterinsurgency in effect since then. Even when the Guatemalan government in 1977 refused U.S. military aid rather than be subjected to human rights review, it still had $15 million "in the pipeline." There were contacts between the Reagan circle and the Guatemalan right wing and military even before the 1980 election. Since the public relations firm Deaver and Hannaford had done public relations for Guatemala during the late 1970s, the Guatemalan power structure had a direct line to the White House, when Michael Deaver was one of the top three White House aides during the first Reagan term.

The Reagan administration has frequently served as apologist for the Guatemalan government. After the March 1982 election, the administration began to speak of President Lucas's hand-picked successor as a "change," only to see a coup on the grounds of electoral fraud. The administration then discovered Lucas's brutal human rights violations, and portrayed Ríos Montt as improving the human rights situation. Reagan stated that Ríos Montt was getting a "bum rap" in late 1982, when mass slaughter carried out by his army was well known. When Ríos Montt was overthrown, his own human rights violations were discovered, and his successor, General Mejía Víctores, was touted as an improvement. On two occasions people employed on USAID (United States Agency for International Development) contracts were murdered either by the army or by persons with army connections. The army resisted all pressure for an investigation. Nevertheless, the Reagan administration continued to press the U.S. Congress to approve increased military aid for Guatemala.

Since the November 1985 election of a civilian president, Guatemala has joined the "democracies." Yet there is every evidence that army control over the country remains as firm as ever. A veneer of democracy may help loosen the purse strings of U.S. aid and may make the Guatemalan military more willing to cooperate with the United States in its strategy in Central America. It will do nothing, however, to solve the underlying problems of Guatemala, which are issues of justice and power.

Some will find Bermúdez's book to be depressing reading. The slaughter he recounts may seem to be a waste, as though it gave witness only to the mystery of iniquity operating with apparent impunity. But Bermúdez clearly intends to share the witness of faith of the poor with the more privileged. Reading with eyes of faith, we can be evangelized, not only by Bermúdez's words but also by the deeds that they mediate.

1

A PEOPLE'S TRAGIC REALITY

The reality of Guatemala, as elsewhere in Central America, is difficult to comprehend unless one has lived it. The misery, hunger, exploitation, and marginalization to which the majority of the people are subjected transport us to a different, totally unimaginable world.

Half-naked, barefoot children, their bellies swollen because of worms or malnutrition, their faces downcast and joyless, are all around us as we move through the mountain villages. Guatemalan children don't laugh. They don't know how. How can you laugh when you see the hand of death over your head?

Guatemala is a rich country—rich in coffee, cotton, sugar cane, and bananas, rich in livestock, rich in fine wood, rich in oil, nickel, and silver. And yet most of the population see only misery, sickness, and death. Why? Because the wealth is concentrated in a few hands. Five percent of the population own 90 percent of the land.

More than 60 percent of the people of Guatemala are Mayan Indians. They are the rightful owners of the land, but they live a life of marginalization, exploitation, and oppression at the hands of a minority of *ladinos*, or whites. The peasant natives live in subhuman conditions, landless, working other people's land for subsistence wages. Truly they are "strangers in their own land."

Illiteracy among the Amerindians in Guatemala tops 84 percent. Only Honduras and Haiti, in Latin America, have a lower literacy rate than Guatemala. And illiteracy opens the sluices to ignorance and exploitation. [1]

Dare to complain, dare to try and change things, and you sign your own death warrant. Every day the bodies of peasant leaders, workers, students, priests, religious, and intellectuals are found in the roadside ditches, cruelly tortured and riddled with bullet holes. Others turn up in secret burial places, crammed into gullies, or even hanging from trees.

How many villages razed, how many villagers massacred! Everyone has heard of the sad events of Panzós, Chajul, Chimaltenango, Coyá, San Cristóbal Verapaz, and so many other massacres. [2]

A report of the diocese of San Cristóbal de las Casas (Chiapas, Mexico) informs us:

> The community of the town of San Francisco had a peaceful life. They had their cornfields and tended them, they looked after their chickens, their children were growing, they prayed, they studied their catechism and were learning to love one another and work as a group. The Army visited the community a number of times and distributed medicine. In fact it promised to help them find a solution to the problem of the land. The people were in peace—but they were gullible. On July 17 the Army came once more, this

time to seize the members of the civil patrols—set up by the government itself—and kill them. Then they surrounded the village and destroyed it, killing children, the elderly, women, and men. Of the 350 inhabitants of the village, somehow, miraculously, 12 survived. The villagers had done no wrong. They had only been gullible.

San Francisco, in Nentón township in the Department of Huehuetenango, was only along the way in the Army's march of destruction and death. The soldiers visited all the villages of the region: Yalcastán, Bulej, Yalanbojox, Trinidad, El Aguacate, Unión, La Cienega, San Antonio, Uxquén, Yalanhuitz, Ixcaxin, San José, and the others. Innocent blood flowed everywhere. Women were raped. The people crowded into their little chapels. . . . Babies were dashed to the ground or swung by their heels against trees to crush their skulls. Children would be told to play, and then, as they tried to obey the order, a grenade would be tossed into the middle of the group. They died playing. . . . A great number of people were hacked to death with machetes, or hanged, or drowned in rivers, or had all their bones broken and were left in the fields. . . . Persons managing to escape were emotional wrecks. They spoke of the use of lethal gases. Wells and streams were poisoned. Corpses were left for the dogs and vultures: there was no one to give them Christian burial.[3]

These are not stories. These are not exaggerations. Testimony abounds. Terror still marks the faces of those who have lived to tell the tale. Witnesses who have lost track of one another in the violence tell the same story.

In Guatemala aspiration for life, the project of life, comes into confrontation with the project of death. Here is the testimony of an Amerindian *campesino* of the Canjobal tribe:

> We were struggling, we natives of the Cuchumatán Mountains. We could no longer bear the poverty of our country. The rich had seized our lands. We were struggling. Some of us no longer even had a place to put a house. Of course there is plenty of land. But the rich own it all, and they no longer give us anything, not even enough to live as human beings, not even enough to live in hunger. We can bear it no longer. And so, you see, we have been trying to fight our way out of this misery. We try to fight for our rights. But the rich crush us, kill us, massacre us, bomb us. . . . You see, the struggle in Guatemala is the struggle of all of us poor. The government says we are Cubans, or from Russia. No, the struggle in Guatemala is the struggle of the poor, of all of us poor, because we are the ones they are killing. If they do not kill us with guns they kill us with the exploitation, hunger, and misery they've kept us in for hundreds of years. So this is why we're rising up now to fight. [4]

In Guatemala, the simple fact of declaring your right to life with its implications—the right to land, health, education, organization, and so on—is a crime, and can get you kidnapped, tortured, and murdered.

A *campesino* or worker in Guatemala does not wonder whether to choose violence or nonviolence. It is not a matter of choice. Like it or not, the violence is there, before your eyes, installed in the government and maintained by North American weapons.

Reports published by *campesino* and worker organizations in Guatemala are full of evidence that all peaceful means for bringing about structural change have been exhausted. This is the situation that has obliged the Guatemalan people to organize for their defense.

The poor do not want violence. They detest it. They long to live in peace. Of course the Guatemalan peasant or worker would like to have peaceful economic and political change. But this is no longer possible. The choice, then, is between starving to death or fighting to live. And the poor of Guatemala, as everywhere else in Central America, have chosen the path of organization and struggle for the building of a new society of justice, peace, and fellowship, with life for everyone.

But the mighty resist this change. Jesus said the rich would not change their minds even if they saw someone rise from the dead (Lk 16:31). Can a camel get through the eye of a needle? It is even harder for a rich exploiter to have a change of heart (Mk 10:25).

Two opposite projects are locked in mortal combat here: the project of life, furthered by the poor, and the project of death, the project of the exploiting rich.

Chiqui was a young Guatemalan everyone knew and loved. She was killed in July 1982. Here is what she had written to her parents from the mountains:

This whole region of Central America is living in a historic moment. Sooner or later it had to come, whether we liked it or not. A whole society has created these huge economic, political, and social contradictions within itself, developing and worsening in recent years and now coming to their climax—to their maximal expression: violence and a dénouement. . . . The Christian principles that you taught us at home and that we learned in school—love of neighbor, justice, community—these are the principles that move us to commit ourselves to our people here and now—to the *campesinos*, the natives, the workers, and the settlers in the outlying districts who are struggling to emerge from such wretched poverty and discrimination.

Guatemalans, an oppressed, believing people, are raising their cry and beginning their struggle, with determination and hope for the project of life.

And this is the reason for the persecution of a church that walks with the people.

2

CHURCH OF THE POOR, CHURCH OF THE CATACOMBS

In July 1980, the diocese of El Quiché was left without priests and sisters, after the murder of a number of missionaries and the machine-gunning of the sisters' convent and the parish hall of Uspantán. Now the catechists and Delegates of the Word of God have assumed responsibility for the process of evangelization that had been begun, and they have done so at the risk of their lives.

In one of the villages of El Ixcán, the community selected as delegate responsible for the administration of the sacraments of baptism and marriage a catechist who could neither read nor write, but who had great moral stature in the community.

Every three weeks the catechists and Delegates of the Word from the various parishes of El Quiché would assemble in a certain place in Alta Verapaz. Some of them would come eighteen hours on foot, often through the mud and rain. One or two would come from each village. They would share their experiences of a church being born of the people.

After the meeting one evening they celebrated Holy Communion, and each one shared his or her experiences with the others. One of them said:

> The word of God says, "Blessed are the persecuted for justice' sake." We used to say, "How nice!" But now that we sense persecution all about us, we see that the word of God is very hard! But yes, this is the kingdom of God.

Another told us he had come a long way, sent by his community to share the Lord's Supper in the name of all. Some wept with emotion at seeing all once more joined together in the Celebration of the Eucharist.

The altar was covered with baskets of bread. After the Mass, each participant came up to take his or her basket home again. Now the bread was Holy Communion for the sisters and brothers of each community, an extension of the Eucharist being celebrated there.

The Delegates of the Word are in practice the Central American version of the deacons in the primitive church, and they discharge their ministry in all fidelity and commitment. Once or twice a week they gather their communities for the celebration or for a planning session on some community development project.

Each celebration begins with an act of reconciliation. In areas where there is no priest, the community celebrates its penance without one. They open the Bible on the altar, and any individual who wishes comes forward to confess his or her sins before the word of God while the community sings an appropriate hymn. In other communities penance is celebrated before the Sacred Host, all who wish coming to the altar to confess their sins.

There are communities where all confess their sins together, aloud, kneeling, everyone at once, then singing a song asking God's forgiveness. Finally the Delegate, in the name of the community, implores God's pardon and mercy upon the whole assembly. Penance celebrations are vital experiences of commitment to conversion, to a change of heart, and they have a strong communitarian dimension.

After the confession, the community celebrates the word of God. The Delegate of the Word reads a passage from the Bible, briefly explains it, and then invites all of the members of the community to voice their comments and express what the reading has meant to them personally.

It is an impressive sight—old and young men and women commenting on the Bible in their own language. Then come the songs, accompanied by guitar, in cowboy rhythm and native style.

Finally, the prayer, which takes a different form in each locality. The Quichés and Cachikeles make their petitions aloud, one after the other. The Kekchies and Pokomchís all pray together—again, aloud, and in their own languages.

When the moment comes for the memorial of the Lord's Supper, the Delegate of the Eucharist gives a short introduction, recalling the meaning of Communion: union with Christ, union with the community, and a commitment to remain steadfast in the faith in this time of persecution and martyrdom.

Then the community repeats the Lord's deed as described in Luke 22 and 1 Corinthians 11, celebrating the Supper commemorating the death and resurrection of the Lord until he comes. Then they receive Holy Communion and give thanks together.

If there is a child to be baptized or a couple to be married, the ceremony takes place at one of these weekly celebrations. The Delegates of the Sacraments, chosen by the community from among the catechists, administer these sacraments, then carry the names of the baptized or newly married to the nearest parish to register them. In some very remote villages, the catechists themselves register the baptisms and marriages, being authorized to do so by the priest or bishop.

Besides conducting the weekly celebrations, the catechists and Delegates serve as chairpersons for conversations, or "chats," as they are called, in preparation for the reception of the sacraments and direct training courses for the whole community on religious subjects or on matters of human and social development.

Soon the Army learned that the church of the people, the church of the poor, was rising up with strength, with commitment to the people's liberation.

Before long the Army ordered the closing of all churches and chapels in the northern part of the El Quiché area, claiming that "there is no reason why everyone should have to pray in the same place at the same time." But native Christians have a strong sense of community. They know full well that Christ is present where two or more are gathered together in his name. Besides, they know that in order to defend themselves from repression and help one another they must remain closely united. So they said, "If they forbid us to meet in the chapels, we shall gather under the trees of the wood or in the caves of the mountains." Others said, "One must obey God rather than human beings, as it says in the Book of the Acts of Apostles." And many continued to meet.

The church had entered the age of the catacombs,

whereupon many Christian leaders were tortured, kidnapped, or murdered. Here is the testimony of Rogelio González, a Protestant Guatemalan refugee who fled the country in 1982 after eight members of his family had been kidnapped:

These bloody, brutal, painful acts carried out by the Guatemalan Army in behalf of the rich and the mighty recall the terrible persecution suffered by Christians in Imperial Rome. There is not a great deal of difference between being thrown to the lions in the Roman Circus and being delivered up in the name of the pagan god Capital to those wild beasts that are the human beings who rule Guatemala.

Like the Christians of old, the people of Guatemala suffer with clenched teeth, with firm reliance on their deep faith. The catacombs of the Roman Empire have become the chill of the mountains of western Guatemala. Hundreds of ministers, priests, sisters, and lay apostles have been murdered. But the Guatemalan regime cannot murder justice, just as the Roman Empire could not murder the message of hope and love of Jesus, the king of kings.

As the Caesars of Jesus' time sought to wipe out hope by means of persecution, in like manner the Caesars of today, in military uniform, try to erase hope by killing the bearers of its message. They are unable to hear the voice of God, calling out from the mouths of the persecuted. They cannot understand that the struggle for justice is not "imported" but springs from the inhuman conditions in which the vast majority of Guatemalan Christians have to live. [5]

3

PERSECUTION AND MARTYRDOM: TESTIMONIALS

The time was November 1980. The persecution and repression of catechists and Christian communities had grown very harsh. Catechists could no longer attend their meetings or carry Holy Communion to their communities without risking discovery by the Army and possible death. So they had to work under cover, pretending that they were only on shopping trips to the departmental capital. One said, "Now we need the Body of Christ more than ever to gain fortitude and strength to struggle side by side with our people."

They would carry the consecrated wafers hidden among ears of corn or in baskets of beans. One morning, as I was vesting for Mass, a catechist appeared out of nowhere and began, timidly, "I beg your pardon, Father . . . but you know we're having a hard time in our community. We want to receive Holy Communion, but if the Army or the Secret Service finds me I'm a goner. So I've got these tortillas here—if possible I'd like to push the Sacred Hosts down inside here." And he opened the napkin covering the tortillas. The faith and simplicity of this person gave me such a lump in my throat I couldn't answer him.

I took the tortillas from my friend and carried them to the altar. After Mass I stuffed a half-dozen hosts down alongside each tortilla. Then I wrapped everything all up in a big cloth and gave it back to the catechist. With the greatest respect and reverence, this good person took the Body of Christ from me and put it in his knapsack. Then he said goodbye and started off back to his community— a two days' walk away, on the other side of the River Chixoy. O Quiché, land of heroes and martyrs!

Because of the leadership they exercise in their communities, Delegates of the Word of God are especially sought out and persecuted by the Army, the Secret Service, and the death squads. They have contributed the greatest number of martyrs among all the pastoral ministers.

On November 12, 1980, government agents entered a village of Chicamán by night. They called at the door of catechist Nicolás Tum Quixtán. He failed to respond. So the agents kicked the door in, entered the house, and found Nicolás by using a flashlight. They attempted to make off with him, but he defended himself as best he could, intent on staying in the house, as he knew that if he were abducted he would be tortured to make him betray the names of the other catechists of the region. As the agents were unable to drag him away, one of them shot him three times. Off went the agents. He fell to the floor and lay in a widening pool of blood. Beside themselves and in tears, Nicolás's wife and mother did not know which way to turn. But Nicolás, his voice distorted with pain, told them: "Kneel down and pray to God for yourselves! You're going to have to suffer a lot. I'm going to die, but I know I'll rise again . . . and take good care of the kids." A few minutes later he was dead.

In the Reina region, on November 19, 1980, some seventy Kaibiles—counterinsurgency specialists of the Guatemalan Army—entered a village by night, in the company of a number of their spies (or "ears," as they are called in Guatemala), used axes to break down the door of the parish church, and tossed a grenade inside. Then they set fire to the houses of five catechists and made off with three of them: Isaías Hernández, his son Mónico, and Manuel Choc. The three were never heard from again. There can be no doubt that they were tortured and killed. A catechist-trainer who had hidden in the mountains saw his little house reduced to ashes—saw the work of so many years disappear in minutes—saw his fourteen-year-old daughter raped, and saw the Kaibiles throw his son to the floor, kick him till he screamed, tie him up, and drag him off. He saw his wife, weeping in the street in helplessness and desperation, protecting her small children from those fiends.

The soldiers went out after this catechist, too, but he succeeded in eluding them. For several days and nights he wandered barefoot in the mountains, with nothing to eat, darting from tree to tree to avoid detection. One evening he appeared in our community, pale and drawn, full of scratches, hungry, despairing, his eyes filled with tears. His face looked as Christ must have looked on the cross. We could only stare at him wordlessly. This was the first time I had ever seen an Amerindian weeping. We did our best to comfort him, then we fed him, and celebrated the Eucharist in company with two more of the brothers who happened to be present. The blood and sorrow of our people were consecrated in the Eucharist that day.

In many regions of Guatemala it is no longer permitted to celebrate the Word. The Bible is considered a subversive book. The Army and the Police send search parties into the villages constantly. If they find a Bible, especially the *Latinoamericana* edition, not only do they take it with them to destroy it, but they make off with the owner as well, whom they accuse of being a communist. Then they kill the person. [6]

Here is what one young catechist had to report:

The soldiers came to our village and searched the houses. When they found Bibles, they ripped them up, stomped on them, and burned them on the spot, before the eyes of their owners and the other catechists. They told them, "If we catch you with one of these again you'll be killed. Get rid of your Bibles."

But the people do not lose their faith that easily. They continue to meet. The young catechist went on:

What some do is bury their Bible and their hymnals. This way they stay out of trouble, and only they know where the books are. Others have to work underground, meeting in little groups so as not to make the government suspicious. They figure it won't make any difference if they're killed as long as they give witness to the Christian faith. They don't care if they're tortured to death; they keep at their work in the community; they keep organizing. They work like priests or sisters—they're the ones who baptize the babies and give communion.

Another catechist:

> You wonder why the government's against the Christians? Because we've caught on to what the Bible's trying to tell us. We see the example of Moses, who led his people out of their slavery. We see the example of Jesus, who was persecuted even as a baby. We compare everything our communities are going through to what went on in those times or to when Jesus was persecuted. Jesus was persecuted by a government. The persecution of the Christians here is so strong because the government knows we're waking up with the Bible and that we're going to keep on waking up. In the Bible we find out what we're supposed to do. [7]

I made a trip to a village in Baja Verapaz, in the township of Rabinal. After the Eucharist a catechist invited me to lunch in his home. There in a corner of his poor little hut on the floor some vigil lamps were burning. I paid no special attention to them, supposing that this was a native custom. But no, those lamps were burning over the hiding place in which the family Bible was buried. This family, like so many others, prayed every day over the Word of God buried under the floor of their house, recalling various passages from memory. If you saw lamps or flowers on the dirt floor of a house, that was a sign that the Holy Book was buried there.

In this same department of Baja Verapaz, one evening a community was gathered for a Celebration of the Word in a chapel near the village of Rabinal—not without fear that the Army might turn up. And so it happened. Some fifty soldiers came and surrounded the chapel. An officer entered, most irreverently, climbed onto the altar, kicked the Bible to the floor, and shouted that this book was "all a pack of lies." Then he gave orders to a soldier to burn it. The soldier strode up, tore the pages out of the Bible with a great show of irreverence, and set fire to them.

The whole community was terrified. In the deathly silence, which was broken only by the sardonic laughter of the troops, the officer read a list of names of twenty-three members of the community, who were also present. These were dragged from the chapel and taken to a house where, without any explanation, they were machine-gunned.

The families of these unlucky ones, crying with anguish and helplessness, did all they could to remain at the victims' sides, but to no avail—the soldiers thrust them back at every turn. It all happened at about midnight. This is from the account of an Amerindian catechist who witnessed the massacre and is presently a refugee in Mexico. [8]

In early January of 1981, the Army entered the village of Macalajau, in Uspantán. The community prepared to flee, and many escaped to the mountains. But the Delegate of the Eucharist, with his wife, headed for the chapel, to rescue the Blessed Sacrament lest the soldiers profane it. They hid it in an earthen vessel, placed the whole thing in a plastic bag, dug a hole in the earth behind the chapel with a machete, and buried it. "They'll kill us," he said. "But Christ will always be in this village."

The catechist was seized and carried off, along with a number of others. Before leaving the village the soldiers put it to the torch, all of the houses and the chapel. They killed the animals, even the dogs. Some women died after being raped. Others, widowed and homeless, wandered with their children to the town of Uspantán. They installed themselves next to the market. It was cold, as it had been raining for days. The Army told the people of Uspantán: "These women are guerrillas—anyone giving them any assistance will be considered to be working for the guerrillas."

Cold and hungry, agonizing and desperate, many of these women, with their children, headed off in various directions, whither they knew not. Several days later fifteen of them were found along a road with their heads cut off. Others reached Alta Verapaz, where one of them told this story:

> There were five of us living in the house—my husband, my three children, and I. I'm the only one left. One evening government soldiers came in, dressed as peasants. They came in unmarked trucks, firing their machine guns. They dragged us all out of our houses. They tied the men to trees, then they raped the women, even little girls nine years old. They said they were guerrillas. Some of the men were dragged away; others were killed on the spot. They slit open the abdomen of a seven-months-pregnant woman with a knife and pulled out the fetus. Then they put her husband's head in her belly. There's nobody left in the village. We're afraid. We're running. We're afraid the Army will come back. [9]

The Army entered the village of Lancetillo during the last week of May 1981. They took Tino Salazar from his home. His daughter Olivia, seeing that the worst was about to happen, asked the soldiers to explain why they were doing this to her father. Unable to help him in any way and desperate, she cried out for help, whereupon a soldier shot her in the head. She collapsed, killed instantly, still clutching her one-year-old daughter to her breast. The baby did not die. Olivia was nineteen. The soldiers burned her hut and seven others. Luckily, most of the people had already fled to the mountains. Some of them managed to get to the rectory in Cobán and report what had happened.

In January 1982, the Army went to San Cristóbal Verapaz. They arrested several catechists, good persons who had chosen to work for the liberation of their people. Four months later, three villages of this township were bombed, and people were massacred in Najtilabaj, Chirexquiché, Las Pacayas, Chituj, and Chisirám—men, women, and children. One hundred twenty bodies were counted. [10]

After the massacres the remaining population fled to the mountains to hide in the forests there. But the Army was not satisfied. They sprayed the mountains with poison gases to exterminate the population, and the Civil Patrol (a military body) poisoned the waters of the wells and streams.

Poor, good people—men and women, young and old—all murdered! Why? You have only to look the people in the eye to discover how much they have suffered. Before it was exploitation, hunger, disease. Now, besides all this, comes repression, fear, anguish, and death.

These massacres are the result of a cold-blooded decision to depopulate certain zones in order to rid them of supposed Guatemalan guerrilla bases. The massacres have caused the flight of two hundred thousand refugees abroad and more than a million to the interior of the country. These massacres are the Army's response to our people's cry for justice and freedom. [11]

Few countries in the history of Latin America have suffered a repression as cruel as Guatemala is suffering. In 1971, during General Arana Osorio's regime, the people living in dozens of villages in the eastern regions of the country were exterminated. [12] An Amerindian former soldier of that regime recounted to us how he had been forcibly inducted and taken to a military post. After a period of preparation he was sent to the eastern part of the country, where soldiers were obliged to set fire to peasants' huts by night, while the people slept inside. He confessed that he would never be able to forget the flame-lit face of a woman trying to flee her home, which had been transformed into a gigantic funeral pyre. "How she looked at me with her great eyes while the fire was burning her house!" The boy found that "mission" one too many. He began to drink, and was eventually discharged from the Army.

During the regime of General Laguerud the massacre of Panzós, in Alta Verapaz, took place. More than one hundred native Kekchi peasants—men, women, and children—were machine-gunned for the sole crime of laying claim to their lands, which were being usurped by the landholders of the region. [13]

When General Romeo Lucas García was in power, terror finally seized all Guatemalans. People were hauled out of the fields or cities in broad daylight. Corpses of those who had been tortured appeared daily along the highways and byways of the land. During Lucas García's regime the persecution of the churches reached its peak. A number of Catholic priests and Protestant ministers paid with their lives for having opted for the poor. [14]

The list of priest-martyrs in Guatemala begins with Bill Woods, a North American. Next to be martyred was the

Guatemalan Hermógenes López, gunned down on June 30, 1978. Shortly before his death, Hermógenes had written: "My crime consists in practicing freedom, every day, and in trying to infect everyone with this freedom, so that they will feel themselves to be persons." The people of Guatemala venerate Hermógenes as a prophet and martyr. [15]

On May 1, 1980, Conrado de la Cruz, a Filipino priest, was abducted, along with Herlindo Cifuentes, a catechist of the community of Tiquisate, in Escuintla. They were never heard from again. Conrado was dedicated to the poor and humble people living along the south coast. Three days after his kidnapping I was having supper in the center house of the Congregation of the Immaculate Heart of Mary, the order to which Conrado belonged. There I met Father Walter Voordeckers, from Belgium, pastor of Santa Lucía in Escuintla. Six days later, on May 12, Father Walter was murdered on his way to church. He was a sincere, simple, deeply truth-loving person.

José María Gran Cirera, a priest from Catalonia, Spain, a Missionary of the Sacred Heart of Jesus, was pastor in Chajul, Quiché, a place notorious for the repression of the *campesinos*. One day he was asked, "José María, aren't you afraid?" And he answered, "Why should I be afraid? Whatever God decides for me will happen to me." A few days later, June 4, 1980, José María was felled by a shot to the heart in a Guatemalan Army ambush, along with his catechist, Domingo Batz.

A group of Guatemalan Christians expressed their feelings about José María's death in this way:

José María was killed because he was a good person, beloved of the people—because he never abandoned his pastoral duty, despite the situation of repression rampant in his region—because he denounced the scourge of the sin of social injustice —because he promoted the dignity of the native campesino—and most of all because he performed his authentic churchly duty, which was to be among the poor and embrace their project of liberation, in solidarity with them in their risks and inevitable persecution, ready to offer the supreme witness of love by defending and helping those whom Jesus loved with a preferential love.

A month later another priest, a Spaniard, of the same congregation, Faustino Villanueva, was killed with two shots to the head on July 10, 1980. He was in his parish office in Joyabaj, Quiché. For over twenty years he had discharged his priestly ministry in the diocese of El Quiché.

In November 1980, Protestant ministers Santos Jiménez Martínez and Jerónimo ("Don Chono") were murdered in the village of La Esperanza, in the township of Santo Domingo, Suchitepéquez.

Santos Jiménez, a sixty-six-year-old campesino, had been forced to leave home at the age of eighteen after a disagreement with his father, a large coffee-plantation owner, over injustices committed against the campesinos. Santos had simply become a campesino himself, joining with his sisters and brothers in their struggle. For him Christian faith was inconceivable apart from a commitment to the struggle for justice. Ecumenist, indefatigable seeker after a new way of "being church," Santos considered that the important thing was to organize to shake off the yoke of oppression and institute a new social order more in accordance with God's plan. Santos was murdered while conducting a religious service in the chapel of his community.

Don Chono, likewise a *campesino* and Santos's inseparable comrade, was his equal in outspoken defense of his brothers and sisters. Possessed of a fine knowledge of the Holy Scriptures, Don Chono was a vibrant speaker. On the night of November 19, as he knelt praying on his mat with his Bible in his hand, Don Chono was murdered.

On May 14, 1981, the Guatemalan priest Carlos Gálvez fell, his body riddled with bullets, on the steps of his church as he was speaking with people of the village.

In June 1981, Jesuit Father Luís Pelecer was kidnapped in broad daylight as he was leaving the Church of Our Lady of Mercy in Guatemala City. For months he was subjected to a clinical torture that finally altered his personality so that he could be used, like a robot, to attack a church committed to the suffering.

In July of the same year, along the road to Quiriguá, Izabal, Franciscan priest Tulio Marcelo Maruzzo was murdered, along with two Delegates of the Word. Father Tulio had been working in the area for more than twenty years. A man of poverty and austerity, he was murdered because he had chosen to work in solidarity with those who suffer, in solidarity with those whose most basic human rights are violated.

During the last days of July 1981, two lay missioners, Raúl Josep Leger from Canada and Angel Martínez Rodrígo of Zaragoza, Spain, fell victim to the assassins' guns. "Angel was a Delegate of the Word, a faithful companion of the *campesino* natives, a cheerful, simple, noble friend who loved us from the heart," said someone who had known him well. In the last letter Angel wrote to his family in Spain he said: "I'm working as hard as I can to be faithful to the Lord, and to the men and women entrusted to me, as I try to 'run the race' with all of the sincerity and dedication that human weakness will permit." Both of them, Angel and Raúl Josep—were killed by the Army in Guatemala City on July 25.

On August 2, 1981, Padre Carlos Pérez Alonso, a Spanish Jesuit, was kidnapped on his way to celebrate the Eucharist in a hospital. The Society of Jesus declared: "We reaffirm our decision to work for the poor and oppressed, despite the risks and the persecution."

Padre Juan Alonso Fernández, a native of Asturias, Spain, had worked for two years in Indonesia and for nearly twenty years in Guatemala. On February 15, 1981, as he was on his way by motorbike from Uspantán to Cunén to celebrate the Eucharist, he was intercepted by police agents and abducted. His bullet-riddled body was found the next day in a ravine.

Father "Francisco" Stanley Rother, from the United States, was murdered in a parish of Santiago Atitlán, Sololá, July 28, 1981.

According to the bishops, Father Stanley had received "word" that he was on the list of those to be killed. He returned to the United States for a time, but the desire to be with his people was too strong, and he came back to Guatemala. The immediate cause of his death may have been his valiant denunciation of the massacre of a group of civilians by the Army in his community of Santiago Atitlán.

In September of the same year, North American missionary David Troyer was murdered. He had been working in *campesino* co-ops in Chimaltenango. He was a person of great faith, and was steadfast in his service to the people. He was very conscious of the exploitation of Guatemala by his native country.

Fray Carlos Morales López, a Guatemalan Dominican, was murdered in broad daylight in downtown Guatemala City in January 1982. He was a simple, direct person, the type who knows how to come out with the truth without any shilly-shallying. One of his confreres gave us the reason for his murder:

He was obsessed by a Christian passion for the integral liberation of Guatemala. And he participated fully in that liberation process. He was convinced of one thing: that the current situation in Guatemala cried out to heaven, that the exploitation in which the agroindustrial and military oligarchies of Guatemala had trammeled his country was unendurable and un-Christian. And so, despite all the risks he knew he was running, he was unwilling to leave Guatemala.

Father Fernando Hoyos, a former Jesuit, a native of Spain, was devoted to the people come what might. He had worked in Guatemala since 1972.

Fernando Hoyos, drawn by his missionary vocation and driven by harsh, inhumane conditions in which the people of Guatemala had to live, had worked long years for the evangelization and education of the Amerindians of the highlands. . . . Oblivious of the personal advantages he might have enjoyed in view of his origin, family position, and intellectual training, he struck his roots among the people of

Guatemala, took their collective aspirations as his own, and devoted himself unstintingly to his tireless work as educator and forger of *campesino* leaders, with the sole objective that they become the architects of the transformations of which the country stood in need.

Here is an extract from a letter Fernando wrote to his friends in the Jesuit order:

From the rain and cold of the mountains, a warm embrace. And the spirit of all my comrades here, all of our concerns and hopes in our struggles, are in this embrace, all run together and overflow. . . . We are still one, you and I, no matter what part of the world we are in. Our problems, our hopes for victory, unite us. . . . We must think that beyond these mountains and these volcanos, across the rivers and the valleys, there are other heads and other hearts in solidarity with ours, feeling the same things as we, suffering and rejoicing as we—and that hope is keen there, too, for a new society of justice and fellowship [October 21, 1981].

Fernando Hoyos was killed on July 13, 1982, in Chojzunil, Huehuetenango.

One of Fernando's comrades recounts that on one occasion as Fernando and some others were on a long trip through the mountains of the Cuchumatanes, some of the group noticed that Fernando was having difficulty walking. He had blisters on his feet and they had broken, exposing the raw flesh. His companions offered to carry him on their backs, but Fernando refused."The suffering of the people hurts me more," he said, and he kept on, his feet bloody.

Another priest killed was Father Augusto Ramírez, a Guatemalan Franciscan, founder of the Christian Youth Movement, a person of God and much beloved by the people. In June 1983, he was arrested by a military patrol and tortured in an army barracks. Six months later, on November 7, he was machine-gunned on his way back from Guatemala City to Antigua, where he was superior of the Franciscan house.

Victoria de la Roca, a Guatemalan nun who worked for the poor in Esquipulas, was kidnapped January 6, 1982, and has not been heard from since. Victoria entered the Congregation of Our Lady of Bethlehem at the age of twenty, and later became aware of the social nature of her country's sufferings. She kept in contact with the popular movements, and was sensitive to the injustices suffered by her sisters and brothers, especially the Amerindians and *campesinos*. At dawn on January 6, her convent was entered by fifteen heavily armed men who attacked the sisters and then burned their convent. They kidnapped Victoria, who was superior of the convent and in charge of the catechetical team of Esquipulas. "Victoria" is both a name and a promise of liberation.

To the number of all of these martyrs must be added an endless list of Delegates of the Word of God, catechists, and Protestant ministers who have borne the witness of the supreme test of love.

More than two hundred pastoral ministers have fled the country because of threats of death or expulsion.

As Scripture promised: *For your sake we are being massacred daily, and reckoned as sheep for the slaugh-*

ter. These are the trials through which we triumph, by
the power of him who loved us [Rm 8:36–37].

The mighty of this earth persecute Christians not because Christians believe in God, but because their faith
leads them to a commitment to justice. By persecuting
them, the mighty seek to slow or halt faith's momentum
for liberation. But this persecution strengthens the faith of
the poor even more, and now they wage their combat in a
church of martyrs.

So many Christians of Guatemala—as of all of Central
America—who have made an option for the liberation of
their people know that they are seeing Jesus' beatitude
fulfilled:

> Happy those who are persecuted in the cause of
>   right:
> theirs in the kingdom of heaven.
> Happy are you when people abuse you and persecute
> you and speak all kinds of calumny against you on
> my account. Rejoice and be glad, for your reward will
> be great in heaven; this is how they persecuted the
> prophets before you [Mt 5:10–12].

Our Christians know that if they compromised with
injustice and corruption—with the death project of foreign imperialism and the national oligarchy—they could
save their lives. For Jesus says:

> If you belonged to the world,
> the world would love you as its own;
> but because you do not belong to the world,
> because my choice withdrew you from the world,

therefore the world hates you. . . .
If they persecuted me,
they will persecute you too. . . .

Yes, they could save their lives. Yet they know that "any-one who wants to save his life will lose it; but anyone who loses his life for my sake, that man will save it" (Lk 9:24).

4

MURDER "IN THE NAME OF GOD AND ANTICOMMUNISM"

After the coup d'état of March 23, 1982, and the coming to power of General Ríos Montt, with his scorched-earth policy, the number of victims of repression rose even higher. [16]

In a year and one-half of his regime, over 15,000 Guatemalans, mostly native *campesinos*, were murdered and massacred by bombing. Dozens of villages have been erased from the map of Guatemala. Only their charred ruins remain. The Ríos Montt scorched-earth policy applied to two-thirds of the national territory. [17]

I transcribe here some of the testimony on the massacres gathered in the report of the Guatemala Justice and Peace Commission on the human rights situation in the country (December 1982). [18]

It was March 30, 1982. The people of the village of Chupol, of the township of Chichicastenango, were gathered in the Protestant church, when the Army entered and demanded to know why they were meeting. "To hear the Word of God," they answered. But the Army accused them of guerrilla activities and specifically of the use of grenades. One of the persons in the church was able to escape, but thirty-six died—men, women, and children. A seven-year-old child who was found alive among the bodies recounted to us what had happened. We ourselves were eyewitnesses of the scene of death the next morning.

The same day, in Chucalibaj, some forty-six people were killed. (Chucalibaj is thirteen kilometers from Chupol.) Wearing camouflage fatigues, the Army arrived and sprayed the dwellings with machine-gun fire. Then they mowed down the people working in the cornfields in the same way. My aunt was in her house preparing the family meal. Her husband and son had fled, for fear of the Army. She had stayed behind, thinking that she and her children would not be harmed. But the Army came and threw a grenade into the house. All were killed. The youngest child was strangled. My aunt was about seven months pregnant. They burned fourteen other houses [Case 19].

The following testimony is from Santa Cruz del Quiché. The events here related occurred at the beginning of April 1982.

On March 23, 1982, the day of the coup d'état, I was in the village of La Estancia, hidden in a ravine and trying to see what we might be able to save of the village. When we heard that Ríos Montt was a "Christian president," we thought our situation might change. But we very soon realized that life would be no different, especially for us Amerindians.

The day after the coup we heard that thirty-five *campesinos* had been killed in Chumatzatz de Sacualpa: seventeen burned alive—soaked in gasoline—the others decapitated. Six of them were my cousins, including a newborn baby and its mother. So we had to hide—the massacres would go on. On April 12, I witnessed the massacres of Chitatul and Xesic, villages of Santa Cruz del Quiché. These little communities were bombed by Army helicopters and planes. More than fifty died and hundreds fled [Case 20].

[Alta Verapaz, June 20, 1982] We had come from the village of Pambach, township of San Cristóbal Verapaz, seeking help, begging an end to the massacre of our children, wives, and aged parents, an end to incendiary raids on our farms that left us without any seed corn. We live on corn. We were desperate now. Armed men had come repeatedly and killed some of us, although we had done no harm. There were not many of us left in the village now, so many had been killed or had fled.

Toward the end of April, soldiers in green-spotted uniforms, all of them armed, came and surrounded our village. Some of the people managed to escape, and headed for the mountains, but the soldiers followed them, caught up with them, and killed them. Ninety-six people were killed in all, mostly children and their mothers, or anyone unable to take flight. Among the dead were many persons from other villages, who had come to live with us because they could no longer continue to live in their communities. Either they had no houses, or no fields, or their families had been murdered and everything burned to the ground. They were afraid that if they went back the Cobán armies would come again and kill them. They did not know where else to turn. We ask you to help us. We ask to be allowed to live in our village without being bombed or having all those death raids. We have no weapons. We ask you to send people from the churches, since Father doesn't come anymore. Maybe they could help us. We have no houses and have been unable to do any planting so we have nothing to make tortillas with, and we have lots of sick children [Case 26].

[A catechist from the parish of Rabinal] July 18 was a day of great sorrow and suffering for many families. They were on their way back from a shopping trip to the market. Along the road they met the Army. A girl who survived told me she'd been with her mother and grandmother when they saw the Army, along the road to the village of Concul. All of the adults, about two hundred people, were forced to enter a certain building. Some of the soldiers were out on the road, stopping the people who came along, others were dragging people out of their houses. They took all these people to the same place.

Then they took the girls and young women to another building, farther away, and when it began to get dark the soldiers came in and started raping them. When the soldiers came out, dragging some of the girls, our witness managed to escape and hide in the woods, in the dark. The next morning she saw no one, so she went to the building to find her mother. She found that everyone had been burned to death. The houses had been burned and the people too. The girl found her mother. She had been burned only half to death, and the girl heard how she wept and screamed, "Kill me, quick!" The girl was so terrified that she ran away, ran past the building where the young women had been, and found them lying all over the hill, shot, along the road and around the building. They were all dead. The girl who told me all this then went to her own house, two hours away on foot. She told her brother what had happened, and he went to see the bodies. He estimated that there were about 250 of them. Some of them had not been burned to death, but had suffocated from being piled one on top of another.

[The witness remarks that this village was now uninhabited, and continues:] When the soldiers had everyone surrounded in this house and set fire to it with gasoline, one girl got away. But the soldiers caught her again, beat her, and left her in terrible shape, with her mouth all torn and bleeding and her tongue split in two. When she tried to defend herself and tell them she hadn't done anything and was just on her way back from choir practice, the soldiers threw what was left of her onto a pile of charred bodies, and made fun of her, praying to God to come and save her and the other dead persons. Hours later, she was found there by her father, who carried her to the village of Rabinal to have her treated. But the soldiers caught him and told him, "If you want to have your daughter treated you're going to have to die yourself." The soldiers wanted to set fire to the girl's clothes because she was a witness. A few days later she died [Case 29].

These are a few of the hundreds of cases in this account.

General Ríos Montt came before the people as an emissary of God. But words have no worth before God if they are not backed up by deeds. These are the deeds of Ríos Montt: towns and villages bombed, fields destroyed, houses burned, wells and streams poisoned, men, women, and children machine-gunned or stabbed to death, kidnappings, torture, and death.

In the face of these acts of death, could Ríos Montt deceive even himself that he was an "emissary of God"? And yet he attempted to justify these acts as part of a "war against communism."

One of the reasons for Ríos Montt's coup was to make it easier for the Reagan administration to send arms to the genocidal government of Guatemala. But when Ríos Montt ceased to be useful to the North American government and became an international embarrassment instead, the United States promoted another coup.

This occurred on August 8, 1983. General Oscar Mejía Víctores took power. Mejía was a hard-line militarist, and as Defense Minister had been directly involved in the massacres perpetrated by the Ríos Montt government. He was completely amenable to the bellicose intentions of the Reagan administration regarding Central America. In the first three months of his administration he murdered more than 3,500 of his fellow Guatemalans, including more than a hundred catechists and one priest. [19]

The Guatemalan military and ruling oligarchy continually try to fool the people with false promises. They have vaunted the elections of 1985 as their new "democratic overture," and they say that those elections demonstrated Guatemalan "freedom and democracy."

Those ignorant of the history of Guatemala will have to be careful not to be taken in by this new ruse. There is no deceiving the people, however. Their long experience in suffering and struggle has taught them to mistrust the mighty.

Among the reasons the military so willingly "turns over its power" to civilians, I cite the following three:

1. At the national and international level alike, the Guatemalan Army has lost a great deal of prestige in consequence of its more than thirty years of criminally repressing the people. And so it is in the interest of the military to see a civilian government installed in order to improve the image of the Guatemalan system.

2. The military is not endangered by civilians coming to power, as it already fields a whole counterinsurgency program that guarantees its retention of all real power. It exercises this power through the inter-institutional coordinating committees, the civil patrols, the model villages, and the development poles. There is no real point in having a civilian government because all actual power is in the hands of the military. The new civilian government will be no more than a democratic facade, a mask for the military to hide behind as it continues to repress and murder the people as it has been doing for thirty years.

3. Finally, the U.S. government pressured the Guatemalan military dictatorship by demanding the installation of a civilian regime as a condition for the resumption of economic and military aid to Guatemala. So-called Guatemalan democracy is a maneuver on the part of Washing-

ton. Furthermore, Washington supports the Christian Democratic Party because it believes it to be the party most likely to support the U.S. policy of intervention in Central America.

Thus civilian government installed in 1986 is part of the Guatemalan military's facade for the world, part of its counterinsurgency plan, and part of the overall Central American strategy of the United States. Who will benefit from the installation of the new government? Only the ruling oligarchy. The people will go on suffering hunger, misery, repression, and death.

These policies and strategies are frequently promoted by persons who call themselves Christians. In December 1983, the Church of Guatemala in Exile addressed a communiqué to the people of the United States, which read, in part:

President Reagan makes use of the name of God to defend his power interest. But Jesus said, "It is not those who say to me, 'Lord, Lord,' who will enter the kingdom of heaven, but the person who does the will of my Father in heaven" (Mt 7:21). But doing the will of the Father means observing his commandment, "THOU SHALT NOT KILL!" God wills respect for human life. And yet the North American government daily fans the flames of war and conflict in the world, and the result is the death of millions of human beings. Is this the will of God? Once again we insist that you are allowing yourselves to be deceived by a government that is sowing the world with death. Listen to the cry of the suffering, which is the cry of God, and you will discover God's will.

God detests those who make use of religion to defend their own interests (Am 5:21–24; Is 1–15).

The mighty consider religion as an ideology capable of keeping people under submission and domination. They confound Christianity with the principles of so-called western civilization.

They speak of God, but they murder God's prophets. Their god is not the God of Jesus. Their god is money. And to this god they sacrifice human lives by the thousands.

They argue that communism is atheistic, that it will destroy religion, and that it is therefore permissible to put communists to death. Actually, the atheists are those who exploit and oppress and make themselves rich off the work of the poor, those whose god is money, and who snuff out people's lives. An atheist is one who denies life and love—for God is Life and God is Love.

5

DRAMA OF OUR TIME:
REFUGEES IN FAITH AND HOPE

Thousands of Guatemalan peasants have run for their lives because of the policy of extermination of the indigenous population in Guatemala. Most take refuge in the desolate mountains of the north, or in the forests, where they live in subhuman conditions, suffering hunger, cold, and disease, eating roots, mushrooms, worms, and plants.

Faced with the alternatives of either fleeing to Mexico or surrendering to the Army and being forced into "strategic villages," these people prefer to resist in the mountains—firmly convinced that one day not very far off liberation will come to their land.

The Guatemalan Bishops' Conference estimated that there are more than a million refugees inside the country, counting both those in the resistance in the mountains and the displaced persons of urban centers.

"Strategic villages" are actually concentration camps run by the Army. Abuse reigns supreme. People kept there live in a structure imposed on them from without and foreign to their culture, in a situation of misery, disease, and degradation.

The hunger and repression that prevail there explain why so many Guatemalan peasants have made such efforts to reach the Mexican border. It is a long journey. The refugees have to hike past the corpses of victims of repression and the ashes of ruined fields and homes. They do not move by day, as they know that many have paid for doing so with their lives. The skies of northwestern Guatemala thunder with military helicopters and planes indiscriminately bombing and strafing any movement of the people. The people must journey by night, with their children and their sick. It is the exodus of the poor. They carry neither food nor any clothing other than what is on their backs.

There have been cases where fathers have swum a river as many times as they had children, with their little ones on their back. Often enough one of the children will be carried away by the current in these crossings. Whole families have drowned. In the mountains, children and the elderly die either of pneumonia (because of the cold and damp) or of dehydration (for lack of water). Mothers have unintentionally smothered their babies to death by holding their hands over the children's faces so that they would not cry when the Army was nearby. A crying baby could mean death for the whole group—the people know this from experience, having seen whole groups of people be killed in attempting to flee to the mountains or the Mexican border.

There are now more than one hundred thousand Guatemalan refugees living in Mexican territory along the eight hundred mile border. Many of them live in extreme misery, under the trees in the forest. Their suffering is being relieved, thanks to the hospitality of the Mexican people and the help of the churches.

No suffering on earth is capable of depriving these people of their faith. Whether under the trees of the forest, in the mountains, or in the refugee camps of Mexico, they celebrate the Word of God as they did in their villages.

Here is the testimony of a religious sister who ministers to refugees in the mountains of Guatemala:

> Our people have not lost their faith in God. On the contrary, their faith is what has helped them to survive, and to hold up during those persecutions and massacres. We have seen burned farms and fields and people wounded by bombs, and the people cry out from the depths of their pain and misery, "My God, my God, why have you forsaken us?" But eventually the awful moments pass, things settle down a bit, and then they happily remember Our Lord's words in Saint Matthew: " . . . I am with you always; yes, to the end of time" (Mt 28:20).
>
> Their faith commits them to their brothers and sisters in love and obligates them to struggle to defend their people and to build a new society in which there will not be so much injustice. In the midst of this struggle, Christians feel the need for God. They cry out to God, they ask the Lord to hear their voice and help them to defend their own lives and those of their brothers and sisters.
>
> The people tell us how prayer has never failed them, how, right from the start, after the Fathers left, they met in homes, passing the Eucharist from family to family, how they prayed there and encouraged one another, how they buried their Bibles so that the

Army would not make off with them, how night after night they would memorize a little passage from the Bible to "keep it in their hearts," get it into their heads forever so they could keep practicing this faith of theirs. They always remembered the priests, and said, "All that they have left us and taught us we shall keep up, right now, right here."

The repression became more severe, and the Army would come at night to kill or kidnap the grown boys and younger men, so that they were always having to run for their lives, toward the mountains. I remember one time I went to a farm. The people who lived there immediately brought out a cassette on which the young people had recorded all of the community's religious songs before leaving for the mountains. The night of their departure the whole community had gathered in the chapel and recorded the voices of all those who were leaving. They brought out that cassette with such reverence. Everyone kept silence as we listened to it. It was a solemn moment. The mothers made their little children keep still so the tape could be heard. That tape was the witness of those who had departed, full of faith, to save their own lives and the lives of the whole village.

Whenever we would go to their little chapels to celebrate our faith publicly, I remember how the people would come along with flowers in their hands, with their vigil lamps, with their smiling faces—you could see they felt the liberation had begun—so happy that they could meet without fear.

By the time we began the celebration the chapels would be full. Those who couldn't get in would be peeking through cracks in the walls or standing on stones or improvised scaffolds outside the door. When we baptized children, everyone wanted baptism all over again. But the most impressive moment for us came when we renewed our baptismal promises—when we promised to be faithful to our Lord, when we said we believed in a God who loves us and whom no one could take away from us, when we promised to keep our faith to the death. The people would spontaneously lift their vigil lamps then, as a sign that they were ready for anything rather than fail their God.

Communion time was another solemn moment. All the people would be crying and singing at the top of their lungs, thanking God either in their language or in Spanish that they had been able to return here to celebrate their faith.

This faith of theirs is not just a feeling or sentiment. It is a whole living witness, shown in the sharing of their tortillas and their little huts with the *Ladinos* (mestizos, non-Amerindians) who passed through the village, fleeing the repression. The *Ladinos* have always looked down on the Amerindians and hurt them. But for Christians there is no inequality of persons, and *Ladinos* are welcomed as if they were Amerindians, and so are foreigners.

And we keep meeting with the people, only it's under the trees now. There we pray, there we encourage one another to keep forging ahead. We haven't any Bibles anymore. Carrying one can get you killed, and besides, we've been running from one place to another. So each person recites a verse from the Bible that he or she especially remembers. One young man said, "Put God's armour on so as to be able to resist" and "stand your ground" (Ep 6:11, 14). At the Prayer of the Faithful the people pray for the oppressors, for those who will be bombing us, that God may grant them a change of heart. I constantly hear prayers for the president, for him to change his life, for his cabinet, for the soldiers, and for the United States government that sends the weapons to the Army that comes to kill us.

Strength like that can only come from God, who will be marching before us in this struggle, who gives us a new heart, without hatred or resentment, who sends the Spirit upon us so that we can find the land of promise and truly be God's people. [20]

One night, in a refugee camp in the south of Mexico, May 13, 1983, I took part in a gathering of more than ninety persons for a celebration of the Word of God. A rude wooden cross driven into the ground, a lamp burning atop a stone, and a little incense in a clay vessel at the foot of the cross were our only liturgical accouterments.

The leader began the prayer service.

"Well, brothers and sisters in the Lord, let's light some more candles and have a little more incense. And now that we are experiencing the persecution the first Christians had to endure, let us pray:

"God our Father, maker of heaven and earth . . ."

" . . . Have mercy on us!"

"Jesus, God of the poor, a God so human and simple . . ."

" . . . Have mercy on us!"

"Holy Spirit, life of our fields and strength for our struggle . . ."

" . . . Have mercy on us!"

"Holy Mary, Our Lady of the Flowers, mistress of our people and our mother . . ."

" . . . Pray for us!"

"Father Bill, first martyr of the church of Guatemala . . ."

" . . . Pray for us!"

Then came the litany of all the priests murdered in Guatemala and an endless list of catechists and members of their communities. Then the people began calling out the name of their local martyrs, and the whole assembly would respond, "Pray for us!" They invoked Archbishop Romero, the great prophet and martyr of Central America.

Then there was a prayer in the Canjobal language, and someone intoned one of the songs the group used to sing in the little chapel back in their village. They couldn't finish. Sobs drowned the song in their throats. After some moments of silence, the leader continued:

"Well, brothers and sisters, I wonder what Jesus would be doing if he were here. I think he would be doing the work we're doing. . . ."

The children slept in their mothers' arms. The martyrs were present and alive that night in that corner of the forest, shining signs of hope.

6

A PEOPLE FIGHTING FOR ITS LIFE

A great deal of blood has been spilled. But this blood is fertilizing the earth. The murder of Christians in Guatemala is so like the death of Jesus Christ.

Now I should like to pay tribute to the memory of five martyrs who gave their lives to deliver their communities from death. Their names: Lucas, Justo, Angel, Domingo, and Juan. They were Amerindian catechists of El Quiché, persons much admired and loved in their communities, true leaders, really at one with their people. But they had directed their activity toward social change. They all proclaimed the Word of God and set up courses of training and conscientization, or consciousness-raising, and they promoted the creation of cooperatives. The task they had taken upon themselves was that of forming and orienting communities in such a way as always to seek to make God's kingdom a real possibility. Government agents saw in these five persons a threat to "national security." [21]

It happened during the first months of General Ríos Montt's administration. One day members of the Army appeared and convoked the entire population of the villages of Santa Cruz El Quiché, municipality of Chesiz. The captain read out the names of these five brothers of ours. They were called up front, and the captain addressed the assembled villagers in the following terms:

> Very well, ladies and gentlemen, these men are subversives. They have to die. Otherwise they'll infect the others. But we won't kill them. The members of their families will. So here are your orders. Choose members of these men's families—their fathers, brothers, sons, uncles—and have them take care of killing these five with machetes. Each family member so chosen is to arm himself with a machete and himself kill his guilty relative. Tomorrow we'll be back—to see how well this order has been executed. If it has not been executed, we'll be back with soldiers and helicopters to bomb every one of these villages. We'll wipe them out. That is all we have to say.

The captain finished, and a deathly silence fell on the assembly. The people looked at one another in terror. No one spoke. Only an anguished silence prevailed. The captain and the soldiers got into their trucks and departed.

Then the people split into groups of twenty-five or thirty to discuss what was to be done with these five persons they all loved so much. The response of all the groups was unanimous, of course. "We won't do it." But when the five catechists took the floor, they stated, firmly: "Brothers and sisters, go ahead and carry out the order. It is better for us to die than for thousands to die."

The people began to weep. The members of the five families were speechless.

It was about four in the morning when the march to the cemetery began. The whole population of the villages took part, men, women, and children. The five condemned persons headed the great procession. All walked in silence, except that you could hear people weeping. They were experiencing in their own flesh the sorrow of Good Friday.

They came to the cemetery. The graves were dug, and the people formed a large circle. The five catechists took their places in the center. One of them prayed the Our Father. All the people prayed it with him. Another said, "We're going to die, but don't worry, we're going to be with God. It's all right to kill us. If we're not killed, our children, our wives, our relatives, and the whole population of these villages will die. Go ahead and kill us."

Another said, "Don't bother about our death. We've done nothing wrong, that's sure. We'll see you in heaven."

Another said, "I only want to ask you one favor. Help my children." The fifth tried to speak too but could not. The tension, sorrow, and anguish were too much. He could only fall to his knees and pray silently. The mothers of some of them, like Mary at the foot of the cross, kept close by their sides.

The terrible moment of crucifixion arrived. The relatives of the five drew their machetes.

The five catechists felt the pain and anguish of death in their flesh. The executioners felt it in their souls. The martyrs were hacked to pieces, and their blood covered the earth, mingled with the tears of the witnesses. All were weeping, some fainted. Here was a mountain of suffering. One of those present went out of his mind.

Their act accomplished, the people wrapped the five

bodies in plastic and buried them. Then they returned home in silence.

On the following day, those charged with informing the Army that its order had been carried out arrived. The military authorities were satisfied. The witness who recounted these events added, "We remember them with holy reverence, because it is thanks to them that we are alive today."

In a similar incident, peasants were obliged to shoot 350 villagers. [22]

These accounts bring to our minds the death of Jesus Christ. Jesus was calumniated and unjustly sentenced to death by the oppressors of his people and the Roman military (Mk 3:6, 11:18, 12:12; Lk 23:1–5, 24:19–20). Our five catechists, who had spent their lives doing good, were calumniated as communists and sentenced to death by the military authorities.

Jesus accepted his death voluntarily, for love of his people (Jn 10:18). These five, too, chose to die to save the entire people. Jesus was accompanied to Calvary by a multitude of the people (Lk 23:27–28). Our catechists, too, walked with all of the people of their villages to the place of execution. Jesus was cruelly tortured (Jn 19:3). The five catechists suffered death by torture, hacked to pieces by machetes. Jesus was sentenced to death as a political rebel, and the crime of which he had been convicted was posted on the cross (Jn 19:19–20). Our catechists were sentenced to death as subversives, political rebels. This was the reason given by the Army.

Once arrived at the place where his anguish was to begin, Jesus entrusted the care of his mother to John, and prayed to his Father to forgive his murderers (Jn 19:26–

27; Lk 23:24). The catechists, just before dying, entrusted the care of their children to the community and prayed the Our Father, in which they said, "Forgive us our trespasses, as we forgive those who trespass against us." No words of hatred or vengefulness were to be heard in their mouths.

Jesus shed his blood to give the gift of life (Jn 10:15). These five Christians shed their blood for the lives of their people too. In life, they had worked indefatigably to improve the horrible living conditions of their communities and had struggled for a new society. Now they bore witness to the authenticity of their love for their people with their deaths.

The martyrs of Guatemala and all Central America, like Christ, are men and women who are part of the concrete life and reality of their people. Through their faith, they discover the social sin of injustice, and bravely commit themselves to the liberation of their people.

Like Christ, they did not want death. They did not go out looking for it. They were persons deeply and passionately in love with life. It was precisely because they could no longer tolerate the system of death that was crushing their people that they risked their lives, finally giving them up for the life of their people. "A man can have no greater love than to lay down his life for his friends" (Jn 15:12–13).

Chiqui, the young Guatemalan mentioned earlier in this little book, five months before her death in July 1982, wrote:

As far as I'm concerned, the only thing I want to do is join the struggle of my people for a better Guatemala. . . . I realize I can die. But what does Jesus say?

"What good is life unless you give it away?" [cf. Mk 8:35]—unless you can give it for a better world, even if you never see that world but have only carried your grain of sand to the building site. Then you're fulfilled as a person.

The martyrs do not die for mystical ideals, nor do they die just to get themselves to heaven. They die because they want life in this world for everyone, because they want a new society.

For the martyrs, faith is the deep motivation of their struggle and dedication to the liberation process of their people. In opting for liberation they know what they are risking. They fear death, as Jesus did (Lk 22:41–44). But their fear does not make them abandon the struggle. Like Jesus, they keep on to the end, battling for life. They accept death as the last resort, the only resort, in their commitment to the struggle for the welfare and life of their sisters and brothers.

Today the poor of Latin America, the Amerindians of Guatemala, are rising up, seeking to shake from their necks the yoke of the oppression they have suffered since the time of the conquistadors. Many Christians are coming to realize that their faith in Christ obliges them to make a commitment to liberation, and so they organize, moved by their faith, which has committed them, in love, to their brothers and sisters. They struggle with determination to change the prevailing system of death, in the hope that one day there will be land, work, bread, housing, health, and education for all—that all may have life in abundance, as Jesus wished for them (Jn 10:10). They seek a new society, where there will be no discrimination against native Americans, where all will have a share in society, be the agents of their own destinies, and so give praise to the God who created them.

Many have already given their lives for this cause. Many have suffered torture or exile. All have struggled and are still struggling in the faith that life is stronger than death and in the hope that blood shed like Christ's blood may bring resurrection to a crucified people.

The struggle of the Guatemalan people for life and freedom is part of the struggle being waged by many Central American and Caribbean people against the oppressive powers that operate in the region.

At this moment in history, the people of Central America are experiencing the agony of Jesus in Gethsemane and on the cross. Jesus seemed a failure. Today his people cry out with him from the cross, "My God, my God, why have you deserted me?" But the cries of an oppressed people reach God's ears and heart (Ex 2).

In Jesus, resurrection became reality because he passed through death.

> Unless a wheat grain falls on the ground and dies,
> it remains only a single grain;
> but if it dies,
> it yields a rich harvest [Jn 12:24].

We may be sure there will be new life for Guatemala and for all peoples struggling for their liberation.

The people are struggling for life. To place oneself in the service of life is to come into confrontation with anti-life—the unjust, oppressive structures that generate death. Capitalism and the National Security ideology operate as the antilife of the people. The oppressor classes call capitalism "democracy," but the truth is that capitalism has nothing democratic about it in Latin American countries like Guatemala. Consequently those who opt for the production of life meet with death, or at least run the risk of doing so. But this death is fecund—like the grain of wheat, which dies in order to yield a harvest.

A long history of *resistance* to foreign domination and *struggle* to change the situation of exploitation and hunger is characteristic of the people of Guatemala and of all of Central America. The effort on the part of the people to build a new society results in persecution and martyrdom. And this is the clearest sign of their triumph. Otherwise what meaning would there be in the death of Christ and of so many martyrs? The church, too, walking with the people in their liberation process, is persecuted. This persecution is unleashed against the church perhaps not out of a direct hatred of the faith but certainly out of a hatred of the consequences of faith—the defense of life, justice, and human worth, or a communion of sisters and brothers that seeks to procure the fulfillment of the plan of God, who created the world for all the sons and daughters of God.

The persecution of Jesus and the prophets was not only by reason of their faith, but also by reason of their activity: denouncing the mighty, the wealthy, and the Pharisees. To give one's life in defense of the life of the people is consciously or unconsciously to give one's life for the God of Life. Neither is the church persecuted for its religious nature. It is persecuted for its defense of human values, without which there is no Christian life. This is why not all Christians, priests, ministers, or bishops are persecuted, but only those who like Jesus have opted for the poor, for justice, and for the life of the whole people.

The gods of inequality, money, and power cannot permit the presence of the God of life and liberty. And so they murder God's witnesses.

In Guatemala, as throughout Central America, a painful, but hopeful, page of history is being written. The blood of martyrs, who already number in the thousands—from the lowliest Christians of the indigenous communities to persons as well known as Archbishop Oscar Arnulfo Romero of San Salvador—is the sign that there will soon be a new society in our lands.

In Guatemala, unlike the case of El Salvador, no prophetic voice has appeared among the hierarchy. But that prophetic voice is in Guatemala in the base Christian communities, among the people.

For love of the people, many persons have joined popular and political organizations, even revolutionary organizations. Many are kidnapped, tortured, and killed in the process. These too are martyrs, whether they are believers or unbelievers, because they could have lived in comfort, or at least in poverty, without risking their lives, but they have opted instead for the path of sacrifice and love of their people.

Others are persecuted and murdered merely for being peasants and Amerindians, merely because they are poor. These too are true martyrs, because they are massacred just for being poor. In Guatemala and in all Central America, being poor is a crime. The very social condition of the poor is a denunciation of the prevailing system of injustice, oppression, and death.

Happy the poor, the persecuted, for theirs is the kingdom of God (f. Lk 6:20–23).

The last of the testimonials presented in this book is one given by the survivor of a massacre:

Narcisa and Lorenza died in the fire, along with 225 other people. They were all burned alive. They were choir members. Lorenza was a long time dying. The soldiers shouted in at them, "Well, get up! Get up if you believe in God."

Well did the high priest say that one person must die for the good of the whole people (cf. Jn 18:14). The words came from the lips of an enemy of Jesus; Saint John interprets them as prophetic. Thus we can interpret the words of the Guatemalan soldiers, too, as a prophecy: "Get up! Get up if you believe in God!" The hour has come in which a people oppressed for centuries is "getting up," is rising up, and no pain or death can break a whole people's longing for liberty and their hope of resurrection and life.

I cannot close this chapter without a call to solidarity.

Solidarity means feeling the pain and the death of our brother or sister in our entrails. God asks us, "Where is your brother . . . ?" And the person without solidarity responds, "I do not know. . . . Am I my brother's guardian?" (Gn 4:9). Those who are indifferent to the blood of their sister and brother make themselves accomplices of the crime of murder (1 Jn 3:15), and will hear God's rebuke: "What have you done? . . . Listen to the sound of your brother's blood, crying out to me from the ground" (Gn 4:10).

As long as there are people who are still miserably poor, exploited, oppressed, massacred, no one can pretend to be a real Christian without suffering with them, without entering into solidarity with them in their struggles and their longings for resurrection.

Solidarity is putting Christian communion into practice. For as Saint Paul reminds us:

If one part is hurt, all parts are hurt with it. If one part is given special honor, all parts enjoy it. Now you together are Christ's body . . . [1 Co 12:26–27].

7

PRAYER OF A PEOPLE IN THE THROES
OF MARTYRDOM

I close these pages with a prayer used by the Christian communities of Latin America. It is the prayer of a people living in the midst of struggle, persecution, and martyrdom, the prayer of those who are in solidarity with the cause of the poor.

Lord, may your Gospel be for me not a book,
    but Good News, lived and shared.
May I not be embittered by oppression.
    May I speak more of hope than of calamities.
May my denunciations be first subjected
      to discernment,
    in community,
    brought before you in profound prayer,
    and uttered without arrogance,
    not as an instrument of aggression,
    but neither with timidity and cowardice.
May I never resign myself to the exploitation of the
      poor,

in whatever form it may come.
Help me to be subversive
of any unjust order.
Help me to be free,
and to struggle for the freedom of the oppressed.
May I never become accustomed to the suffering
of the martyrs
and the news that my brothers and sisters are
enduring persecution,
but may their lives and witness ever move me to
conversion
and to the greatest loyalty to the kingdom.
May I accept my church with an ever growing love
and with Christian realism.
May I not reject it for its faults,
but feel myself committed to renew it,
and help it to be what you, Lord, want it to be.
May I fear not death, but infidelity.

NOTES

1. *Naturaleza y alcance de la pobreza en Guatemala,* CEPAL (UN), Doc. 2, April 1981; "Guatemala: The Roots of Revolution," *Special Update,* February 1983 (Washington Office on Latin America), p. 2.

2. "Villages and settlements that have simply disappeared from the map number in the hundreds" (*Situación de los derechos humanos en Guatemala, 1983* [Comité Pro Justicia y Paz de Guatemala]: "Arrasamiento" ["Demolition"], p. 90. See also *The New York Times,* October 12, 1982; R. Falla, "The San Francisco Massacre," *American Anthropology* (December 1982); Eduardo H. Galeano, *Guatemala: un pueblo en lucha* (Madrid: Revolución, 1983); *Situación de los derechos humanos,* pp. 101,102; "Setecientos campesinos relatan la represión en Tzeja," *Excélsior* (Mexico City), February 6, 1983; "Fue totalmente arrasada una villa guatemalteca," ibid., January 7, 1983, p. 2a.

3. Bulletin of the Christian Solidarity Committee of the diocese of San Cristóbal de las Casas, August 1982.

4. "Testimonio del Via Crucis del Pueblo de Guatemala, 1982," *Revista Anual* (Madrid).

5. Rogelio González, "Replaying Rome in Guatemala," *Third World Sermon Notes* (Madison, Wisconsin: The Presbyterian Church, October 21, 1984).

6. The *Biblia Latinoamericana* is one of the most popular Bibles in Latin America, and has pictures and text explanations and discussions that foster critical thinking. Possession of a Bible in Guatemala is practically suicide: See *Excélsior,* March 7, 1983, p. 34a. The situation in El Salvador is similar, as we hear from Emelina Panameño de García, the Salvadoran who went

to Washington, D.C., as representative of the group "Co-madres" to receive the Human Rights Prize in November 1984. See also *Excélsior*, November 27, 1984, p. 26a.

7. Testimony at the Madrid session of the Peoples' Tribunal, "Sentence against Guatemala," *Uno más uno* (Mexico City), February 6, 1983.

8. Testimony before the Peoples' Tribunal in Madrid in January 1983. Members of the jury included Nobel Peace laureate Adolfo Pérez Esquivel, Bishop Sergio Méndez Arceo of Mexico, and Protestant theologian Harvey Cox (*Noticias de Guatemala* [Mexico City], February 1983).

9. *Interviu* (Spain), July 1981.

10. *Boletín "Coyuntura"* (Costa Rica), 1982.

11. The bishops report the extent of violence and injustice in Guatemala: more than one hundred thousand persons murdered by the government (*Excélsior*, September 5, 1984, p. 2a).

12. Susanne Jonas and David Tobis, comp., *Guatemala: una historia inmediata*, produced by the members of the North American Congress on Guatemala (Mexico City: Siglo Veintiuno, 1976), p. 343. Cf. Susanne Jonas, ed. and trans., *Guatemala: Tyranny on Trial: Testimony of the People's Tribunal* (San Francisco: Synthesis, 1984). See also Galeano, *Guatemala: un pueblo en lucha*, p. 39.

13. Rafael Mondragón, *Guatemala* (Mexico City: COPEC/CECOPE, 1983), p. 16.

14. Catechist Vicente Menchú was burned alive along with other *campesinos* in the Spanish embassy in January 1981. See "Reflections of the Centenary of Evangelical Work in Guatemala," in the bulletin published by North American citizens in Mexico, March 1983; Pedro Caalix, "Testimonies of the People of God," *Communion* (Philadelphia: Fellowship of Evangelicals for Guatemala), July 1983, p. 3.

15. His name is on a 1978 commemorative plaque of the Committee for Justice and Peace of Guatemala.

16. *Situación de los derechos humanos en Guatemala*, "Arrasamiento" (1983), pp. 12, 90.

17. "Genocidio contra indígenas de Guatemala," *Excélsior*, February 24, 1984.

18. These cases appear in the 1982 report of the Comité Pro Justicia y Paz de Guatemala.

19. See the address of Mejía Víctores in Communiqué no. 68 (August 8, 1983) of the Secretariate for Public Relations of the Office of the President of the Republic.

20. *Christus* (Mexico City), April–May 1982.

21. *Situación de los derechos humanos*, pp. 43–50: "Plan Nacional de Seguridad y Desarrollo."

22. *Uno más uno,* March 9, 1983, p. 11.